Julian Press

# The Treasure of Blackbird Rock and Other Mysteries



cbj

© privat

## DER AUTOR

Julian Press, Jahrgang 1960, studierte in Hamburg an der Fachhochschule Grafik und Illustration, hat in einem Jugendbuchverlag volontiert und war dann für Jugendzeitschriften und in einer Werbeagentur tätig. Schon bald begann er, selbst für Kinder zu schreiben und zu zeichnen. Er trat früh in die Fußstapfen seines Vaters, Autor der berühmten »Schwarzen Hand«, und begann, eigene Ratekrimis und Wimmelbilder zu entwerfen. Nach längerem Aufenthalt in Brüssel lebt er heute mit seiner Frau als freier Grafiker und Autor in Hamburg. Seine sehr lebendigen, interaktiven Lesungen sind bei kleinen und großen Spürnasen sehr beliebt.

Julian Press

# The Treasure of Blackbird Rock and Other Mysteries

Mit einem Vorwort
und Vokabelhilfen
von Birgit Hock

cbj

cbj
ist der Kinder- und Jugendbuchverlag
in der Verlagsgruppe Random House

FSC
Mix
Produktgruppe aus vorbildlich
bewirtschafteten Wäldern und
anderen kontrollierten Herkünften

Zert.-Nr. SGS-COC-1940
www.fsc.org
© 1996 Forest Stewardship Council

Verlagsgruppe Random House FSC-DEU-0100
Das für dieses Buch verwendete FSC-zertifizierte
Papier *München Super Extra* liefert Arctic Paper
Mochenwangen GmbH.

1. Auflage
Erstmals als cbj Taschenbuch Juni 2009
Gesetzt nach den Regeln der Rechtschreibreform

Übersetzt und bearbeitet von Miller Literary Agency,
LLC. Erschienen 2008 unter dem Titel
»Get a Clue: The Treasure of Blackbird Rock.
A Picture Mystery« bei Grosset & Dunlap
(a division of Penguin Young Readers Group, USA).

Umschlag- und Innenillustrationen: Julian Press
Umschlaggestaltung: Basic-Book-Design,
Karl Müller-Bussdorf
Vorwort und Vokabelhilfen: Birgit Hock
MI • Herstellung: CZ
Satz: Uhl + Massopust, Aalen
Druck und Bindung: GGP Media GmbH, Pößneck
ISBN: 978-3-570-22056-6
Printed in Germany

**www.cbj-verlag.de**

Liebe Leserin, lieber Leser,

ganz viel Rätselspaß – das bieten dir die vorliegenden Seiten. Warum? Nun, zum einen kannst du mit den Detektiven Caro, Philipp und Flo die vier Geheimnisse aufspüren, denen die Bande in diesem Buch auf der Spur ist. Da geht es darum, das Geheimnis des vierzehnten Mönches zu entlarven und einem Kaninchendieb auf die Spur zu kommen. Und zum anderen kannst du dir einen Spaß daraus machen, englische Vokabeln zu erraten – und zwar so:

- Im Text der Geschichte sind manche Wörter **fett** gedruckt – das sind Wörter, die du vermutlich nicht kennst. Damit du aber trotzdem verstehst, was du liest, ohne ständig jemanden fragen oder in einem Wörterbuch blättern zu müssen, hat dieses Buch Vokabelleisten. Sie führen dich also stets auf die richtige Spur – du verstehst sofort, worum es geht, und der Spaß an der Geschichte (und am Lesen!) bleibt erhalten!

- Damit du solche neuen Wörter in eigenen Sätzen und Situationen verwenden kannst, steht immer die Grundform da (z.B. der Infinitiv eines Verbs) – schließlich lernst du schon lange genug Englisch, um z.B. Vergangenheitsformen zu erkennen bzw. selbstständig zu bilden.

- Sicher aber stolperst du auch über Wörter, die nicht fett gedruckt sind, obwohl du sie nicht verstehst. Nun kommt dein Spürsinn zum Einsatz! Überlege, welches deutsche Wort in diesem Satz Sinn machen würde, und lies die Geschichte dann einfach weiter, ohne die Vokabel nachzuschauen. Du wirst merken, dass deine Vermutung in den meisten Fällen richtig ist. Denn: Auch der beste Detektiv hat nicht immer gleich handfeste Beweise in der Hand, oft muss er sich erst einmal auf seine Vermutungen stützen ☺!

- Manche Wörter kennst du vielleicht eher aus Spielfilmen oder aus dem Internet statt aus dem Schulunterricht: In den meisten Fällen wird es sich dabei um sog. Amerikanismen – also Begriffe, die aus dem amerikanischen Englisch stammen – handeln.

- Amerikanismen sind im Text übrigens auch markiert und du findest die entsprechenden Vokabeln des Britischen Englisch (BE) dort angegeben. Für den Fall, dass Ermittlungen dich auch mal nach Großbritannien führen!

- Und nun: Verlass dich auf deine Intuition – lies einfach drauflos! Dein kriminalistischer Durchblick und dein scharfer Verstand lassen dich ganz bestimmt auch die Klippen der Fremdsprache umschiffen!

Viel Spaß!

The Sugar Shack sold the best **candy** in Hillsdale, the **tiny** town where best friends Flo, Philipp, and Caro lived. The Sugar Shack was owned by Caro's uncle, Leo. Caro and Flo spent a lot of time there after school. Sometimes Caro's other uncle, Lars, **dropped by**. Lars **was** a police detective and **a sucker for** lollipops. The three friends loved mysteries, **suspense** stories, and solving puzzles, so they constantly **harassed** Lars with questions about his work. One day Lars suggested they start up their own detective agency. They could use the candy **storage room** in the attic of the Sugar Shack as their headquarters, and Leo and Lars could be their technical consultants. The three friends jumped at the chance! It was no time at all before they solved their very first case...

**candy:** Süßigkeiten (BE: sweets); **tiny**: klein, winzig; **to drop by:** kurz vorbeischauen; **to be a sucker for:** eine Schwäche haben für; **suspense:** die Spannung; **to harass:** belästigen, nerven; **storage room:** der Lagerraum

**Leo,** the owner of the Sugar Shack, is like some of the chocolates he sells: tough on the outside, **gooey** on the inside.

**Flo** (short for Florentin) has eagle eyes and loves **gadgets**. His pockets are always full of tools to use in unexpected situations.

**Caro** (short for Carolin) is extremely athletic. She's fast and **competitive**. She loves a good **challenge**.

**Inspector Lars** is a computer whiz. He gave his old computer to the detectives, who sometimes use it when working on a case.

**Philipp** has a sensitive ear, especially for birdcalls. The clucking of his loyal **cockatoo**, Coco, is like a second language to him.

**Coco the cockatoo** is Philipp's **sidekick**. More than one criminal has **gotten into a flap** with Coco's wings.

**gooey:** zäh; **competitive:** kämpferisch; **challenge:** die Herausforderung; **cockatoo:** der Kakadu; **gadget:** die technische Spielerei; **sidekick** (*coll.*): der Kumpel, der ständige Begleiter; **to get in a flap** (*coll.*): in helle Aufregung geraten

You can help Caro, Philipp, Flo and friends solve the mysteries in the book. Just read the stories, and try to answer the questions. Here's a hint: Look at the pictures for clues!

# 1. Seven Little Blackbirds

It was a hot June morning when a group of sixth-grade students from Hillsdale Middle School left for a field trip. Their destination: the **Abbey** of **Blackbird** Rock. Caro, Philipp and Flo were among the students in attendance. Their social studies teacher, Mr Johnson, even let Coco, Philipp's cockatoo, come along.
The bus wound its way through the pine forest on the way to the abbey. Philipp felt **woozy**, so he rested his head against the window. When he heard a chorus of »Oohs!« and »Aahs!« from his classmates, he quickly opened his eyes. There it was! The huge stone **monastery** appeared on a plateau in the distance.

The Abbey of Blackbird Rock was made of gigantic stones and its walls were covered with **ivy**. The deafening **caws** of a flock of blackbirds **perched** on top of the bell tower greeted the children as they descended from the bus. Father Anselm greeted the children and took them on a tour.
»According to legend,« he began, »seven blackbirds guided Brother Roger to this rock. The abbey was named for the birds, and seven of them have watched over it since its construction ...«
»Oh no,« Father Anselm interrupted himself, »I only see six!«

**abbey:** das Kloster, die Abtei; **blackbird:** die Amsel; **woozy:** benebelt; **monastery:** das Kloster; **ivy:** der Efeu; **caw:** das Krächzen; **to perch:** sitzen; **medieval:** mittelalterlich (BE: mediaeval)

**Where was the seventh blackbird?**
**Flo knew where it was.**

# 2. Father Anselm's Second Surprise

Father Anselm calmed down once Flo pointed out the missing blackbird. The bird was hiding behind the **broom** that leaned against the left tower wall.

»Silly bird,« Father Anselm cried. »Go join your brothers!«

Then he guided his visitors into the majestic abbey **sanctuary**. Daylight streamed through the colourful stained-glass windows into the **vast** center **aisle**, reflecting red, blue, green, and gold onto the tile floor. He waited for the small group to reassemble around him before continuing his speech.

»Can you see the great stone pillars on each side of the aisle, children? Go ahead, try to put your arms around them.«

The children rushed to encircle the **pillars**; it took no fewer than six to surround each one.

»These pillars alone,« explained Father Anselm, »support the weight of the **vaulted** ceiling, which appears so light. Creating a vast space that defies the law of gravity required incredible ingenuity –«

He interrupted himself again, shocked. The door to the garden outside was **ajar**, even though access was strictly prohibited! Philipp went over and looked out through an arched window. Father Anselm definitely had reason to worry!

**broom:** der Besen; **sanctuary:** der Altarraum; **vast:** riesig; **aisle:** der Gang; **pillar:** der (Gewölbe-)Pfeiler, die Säule; **vaulted:** gewölbt; **ajar:** angelehnt

**What out-of-place object did Philipp discover in the garden?**

# 3. The Dormitory Discovery

**P**hilipp saw it right away: There was a key lying at the foot of the **shrub** in the opposite corner of the garden. This meant that someone had gone into the garden through the abbey, despite the big sign on the front of the door announcing that access to the garden was strictly forbidden during renovations. Philipp signalled his discovery to Caro and Flo.

When the field trip was over, Mr Johnson and the students left – all except Philipp, Flo and Caro, whose research project, by happy coincidence, was on the topic of monastery **herb gardens**.

Father Anselm showed them the library, which contained botanical books that would be useful in writing their paper. Then the friends had lunch with the thirteen monks who still lived in the abbey. The meal passed in silence, but this didn't stop the three detectives' **investigative wheels** from turning. Who went into the garden? And why?

Throughout the meal, Caro had been keeping an eye on the southern wing of the abbey where the monks' sleeping quarters were located. Suddenly, she leaned in toward her friends.

»There's someone in the **dormitory**,« she whispered.

**shrub:** der Busch, der Strauch; **herb garden:** der Kräutergarten; **investigative wheels:** hier: der Spürsinn; **dormitory:** der Schlafsaal; **intruder:** der Eindringling

**What made Caro so sure of the presence of an intruder?**

# 4. Midnight Mayhem

The gang told Father Anselm that they thought someone was **prowling** through the dormitory of the south wing. The detectives saw that the blinds of the window on the far right-hand side of the second floor had been lowered over the course of lunch. Quickly, Father Anselm took a count of the monks. All thirteen were present. Who, then, was prowling through the dormitory of the south wing?
When Father Anselm went to the dormitory to investigate, there was no one there. On the way back to lunch, he couldn't stop himself from smiling. These kids had big imaginations, but maybe they were just a little too big. He couldn't believe that he had fallen for their game! He **scolded** himself.
But then again, how could he explain the key in the garden? Father Anselm sighed. Maybe the brother in charge of the garden, who tended to be forgetful, had dropped his key.
Father Anselm showed the three friends to a monk's cell, which would be their guest room for the night.
»We wake at **dawn,**« said Father Anselm. »Sweet dreams!«
The detectives tried to sleep, but they couldn't stop thinking about the mystery. As the abbey's bells **chimed** midnight, Caro heard voices coming from the garden. She woke the others. They dressed quickly and crept downstairs. After a few minutes, the friends were almost ready to go back to their cell when Flo pointed his finger at something moving in the shadows.

**mayhem:** das Chaos; **to prowl:** herumstreichen; **to scold:** schimpfen; **dawn:** die Dämmerung; **to chime:** läuten



? **What caught Flo's eye?**

# 5. The Key to Success

**W**alking on their **tiptoes**, the young detectives approached the small staircase at the back of the garden. The sandals that Flo had spotted in the shadows underneath the stairs were attached to a person! It was one of the monks lying on the ground, tied up with a cord.

»He's alive!« Philipp whispered. »He's just **unconscious**.« Flo ran for help. Minutes later, he returned with Father Anselm.

»Goodness!« Father Anselm shouted. »Help me lift him!«

They carried Brother Bertram to the **infirmary**, where he started to regain **consciousness**. He was groaning: »I was studying in the library when I heard glass breaking outside. I ran toward the square tower and saw a silhouette moving in the darkness. It was a man in a **robe**. He knocked me over, put his hand over my mouth, and dragged me to the ground ...«

Brother Bertram was exhausted. While Father Anselm rubbed Brother Bertram's **temples** with a **balm**, the three friends **ducked out** of the room. As Philipp headed for the door, he spied a set of keys that Father Anselm had left on the table. He discreetly slipped the keys in his pocket.

The kids used the keys to inspect each room. Finally, on the third floor, they discovered something. Brother Bertram's **assailant** had been here!

**tiptoe:** die Zehenspitze; **unconscious:** bewusstlos; **infirmary:** das Krankenzimmer; **consciousness:** das Bewusstsein; **robe:** das Mönchsgewand; **temple:** die Schläfe; **balm:** der Balsam; **to duck out:** sich davonmachen; **assailant:** der Angreifer



**What detail proves it?**

1727

# 6. The Stranger Didn't Take the Stairs

**A** careful examination of the office **revealed** that the cord of the curtains on the window was torn off. Brother Bertram had been tied up with the missing part of the cord.
Father Anselm caught up with the kids and gasped when he entered the room. He **stammered** and pointed. The three friends turned to discover the source of his **distress**. The safe! Its door was wide open!

»This safe is where we keep our most ancient and precious liturgical objects,« he explained. »Philipp, if I may have my key ring back, please.«
Father Anselm verified that the key to the room and the key to the safe were still on his keychain. How could the thief have entered the room if the door was locked?
»I've got it!« exclaimed Philipp. »Do you see the broken glass? Whoever broke in came in through the window in the back of the room after breaking one of the panes.«
»Really?« asked Flo. »And how did he break in through a window on the third floor? I don't see a ladder.«
Philipp didn't have an answer. The three friends helped Father Anselm take an **inventory** of the safe and then they went back to their cell. Caro opened the **skylight** of their room and **popped** her head **out** to look at the area surrounding the square tower.
»Come and look. I think I've found how the thief reached the third floor!« she exclaimed.

**to reveal:** offenlegen; **to stammer**: stammeln; **distress:** die Verzweiflung, das Elend; **inventory:** die Bestandsaufnahme; **skylight:** die Dachluke; **to pop out:** hinausstrecken



? **How did the thief break into the third-floor room?**

# 7. A Needle in a Haystack

**A** rope was tied to the chimney of the square tower. It seemed that the thief had reached the third floor by flinging up a **grappling hook**, then scaling the side of the tower to the window.

»Look!« said Philipp. He pointed to a man dressed as a monk running through the garden.

»That's definitely not Father Anselm. I can see Father Anselm in the window of the tower,« said Flo. »And it isn't Brother Bertram. He's too **banged up** to run. Who could it be? And what is he carrying under his arm?«

»That's what we're going to find out,« said Caro, rushing toward the stairs. »Come on. Hurry up or he'll get away again.«

Just as Caro entered the garden, she saw the suspect head for the forest, where he **vanished** instantly.

»I don't know if you noticed –« Caro began.

»That he wasn't carrying anything?« interrupted Philipp. »If only we knew where he hid whatever he was carrying.«

»I know,« announced Flo, rather proud of himself. »Follow me.«

**haystack:** der Heuhaufen; **grappling hook:** der Schraubhaken; **to be banged up:** mitgenommen sein; **to vanish:** verschwinden; **to stash:** verstauen, verstecken; **loot:** die Beute

**Flo's photographic memory comes in handy at times like these. Where did the thief stash his loot?**

# 8. The Fruits of Their Labors

Flo ran toward the **potted** lemon tree in the garden. When he had seen the tree earlier from the window of the guest room, he had noticed that the lemon hanging from the tree's branch was on the right, and now it was on the left. Flo concluded that in the time it had taken the kids to reach the garden, the intruder had moved the lemon tree. But why? Flo was pretty sure he knew the answer.

»Come help me,« he said. »I think we'll find a surprise.«

The friends moved the lemon tree and discovered a plastic bag with a heavy object inside behind the pot. Flo plunged his hand into the bag and found a beautifully decorated silver **chalice**. It looked like it had to be one of the treasures that Father Anselm kept in the safe.

»But how did you know it was there?« Caro asked.

»Simple powers of **deduction**,« Flo responded proudly.

Father Anselm was very happy when the young detectives returned the stolen chalice to him. As a **reward**, he let them visit the library where the monks were spending the morning. Flo, Philipp, and Caro were so tired from mystery-solving the night before, they could hardly keep their eyes open.

Caro rubbed her eyes to try to stay awake. No, it wasn't possible!

»The thief is here,« she whispered to Flo and Philipp. »See for yourselves!«

**potted:** im Topf; **chalice:** der Abendmahlkelch; **deduction:** die Schlussfolgerung; **reward:** die Belohnung

**What made Caro so sure?**

# 9. A Prediction

Caro counted up the monks and realized that there was one monk too many! When the **phony** monk realized what Caro had discovered, he dropped his books and **bolted** away. He quickly disappeared behind a door at the back of the room. Caro ran after the man and slipped behind him just before the door closed.
The secret passage was **damp** and **musty**. Caro heard someone panting in the darkness. She flattened herself against the wall, her heart racing. Then she let out a scream: Something was running along the side of her cheek. A spider? A **cockroach**? She rubbed her hands all over her face. Suddenly a door opened at the other end of the passage, letting in a sliver of light. Caro saw the **imposter** disappear through the door and into the church. She was ready to take off after the thief again, but a hand on her shoulder stopped her. Father Anselm had caught up with her.

»Stop!« he said. »This isn't a game. Caro, you and your friends are great detectives, but this could be dangerous. I'm going to call the police, and you should go and rejoin your friends.«
Caro found Flo and Philipp, and the three detectives waited until the monks had left to investigate the crime before they snuck back into the church. But it was too late. The thief was gone.
»The man passed through here,« Flo said as the group walked through a thin, tall doorway. »And I'm certain he's really annoyed right now.«

**prediction:** die Vorhersage, die Prophezeiung; **phony:** falsch; **to bolt:** sausen; **damp:** feucht; **musty:** muffig, modrig; **cockroach:** die Kakerlake; **imposter:** der Betrüger



**What clue had not escaped Flo?**

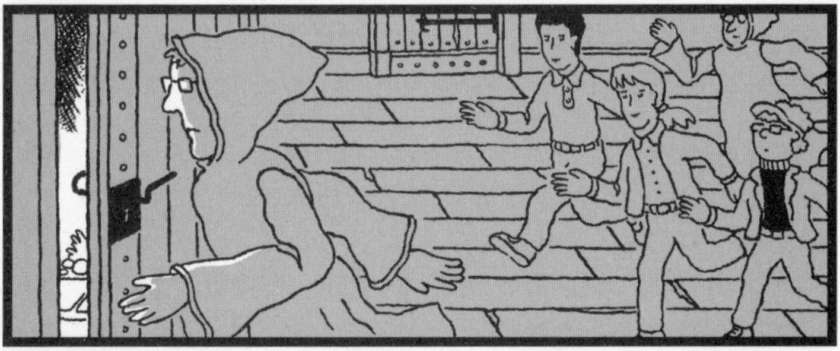

1811

# 10. Keep Your Eyes Peeled

The thief had accidentally dropped his glasses at the foot of the window on the right. Flo knew from experience how annoying it was to lose your glasses!

»I wonder why he risked mixing with the monks in the library,« Philipp said. »He knew we had discovered the theft and found the chalice.«

»Precisely,« said Father Anselm, who appeared suddenly, carrying a bucket of water in his hand. »That's why he came back. The man was desperate to get back our valuable silver chalice. Somebody probably paid him a large sum of money to steal it. These kinds of thefts happen all the time, unfortunately. What can we do besides **alert** the police and lock up the chalice again?« He sighed. »After lunch, children, I'd like you to water the vegetable garden. I hope that will take your mind off of all this **unpleasantness**.«

As soon as they finished eating, Flo, Philipp and Caro went to the **well** to get water for the vegetables. After they completed the **chore**, they considered rolling up their **pants** and wading in the shallow well to cool off. Before they could, Philipp spotted another clue.

»The thief is over there,« Philipp told his friends. »I'm sure of it. And this time, we've got him **cornered**!«

**to alert:** alarmieren; **unpleasantness:** die Widerwärtigkeit; **well:** der Brunnen; **chore:** die Pflicht, die Aufgabe; **pants:** Hose (BE: trousers); **to corner:** in die Enge treiben



**Where was the thief hiding?**

# 11. Another Miscount

Only the most brilliant detective would notice the detail that Philipp had picked up: The wheel of the wheelbarrow at the back of the garden was flat! There was something heavy in it, weighing it down. Because of the theft, no one had worked in the garden all day, so it couldn't have been the monks who loaded it up – it had to be the thief. He was hiding in the wheelbarrow!
Alerted by Father Anselm's call, Inspector Lars arrived at the abbey with Leo. Caro brought her uncles up to speed.
»Police!« Lars announced and pointed to the wheelbarrow. »Come out with your hands up. You're trapped!«
The thief realized there was no way for him to escape. He surrendered and Lars put the **cuffs** on him. The three detectives ran back to the abbey to tell Father Anselm their news. The other monks told them that Father Anselm had just gone up to his room for his afternoon nap.
On their way up to Father Anselm's room, the detectives stopped to help Brother Claudius hand out tickets to a large group of tourists. They collected ticket **stubs** and herded the tourists into the church, where Brother Claudius planned to give the group a short history of the abbey.
But as the visitors **assembled** in the church, Caro had a terrible realization.
»One of the tourists is missing!« she cried.

**miscount:** der Rechenfehler; **cuffs** ( = hand cuffs): die Handschellen; **stub:** der Abschnitt, Abriss; **to assemble:** sich versammeln

**Which of the visitors decided to take his own private tour?**

TOUR ST CAPES

# 12. Time Is Running Out

Philipp and Flo quickly counted the visitors to whom they had given tickets. Caro was right. The man in the hat carrying an umbrella wasn't there! They had to tell Father Anselm right away. While Brother Claudius told the visitors the history of Blackbird Rock, Flo, Philipp, and Caro climbed up the stairs and along the **passageway** that led to Father Anselm's cell. They knocked on the door, lightly at first, but then louder and louder.

No answer. Where was he?

»I think I hear groaning, don't you?« whispered Caro. **Goosebumps** appeared all over her long arms.

Even though he was afraid, Philipp pressed his eye up against the keyhole and squinted into Father Anselm's room.

»Come on, tell us what you see in there!« Flo said urgently.

»I … I don't know. I think Father Anselm is in danger. In any case, he or someone else is certainly in his room. Look for yourselves!«

**passageway:** der Durchgang; **goosebumps:** die Gänsehaut

**What proved that someone had recently been in the room?**

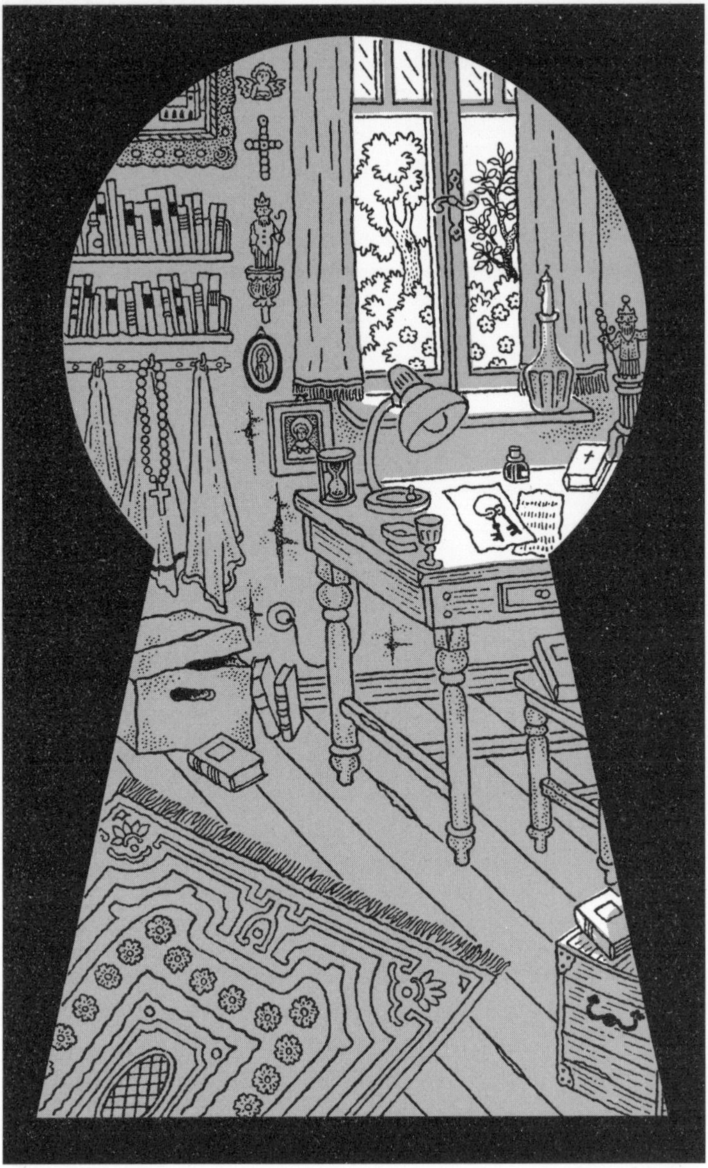

# 13. The Phantom Patient

After taking turns looking through the keyhole, Caro and Flo saw the **evidence** for themselves. The hourglass on the desk had been turned upside down just a few minutes earlier. **Grains** of sand trickled slowly into the bottom of the hourglass. Someone must have been there recently to turn the hourglass.
The three friends ran to the kitchen, where Brother Donald was busy making dinner. Once he heard the news, he hurried to unlock the door to Father Anselm's room.

»Oh no!« he exclaimed when he saw poor Father Anselm tied to a chair in the corner of the room with a sock stuffed into his mouth. Who could have done this?
»Thank goodness you came to look for me!« Father Anselm gasped. »I went to turn over my hourglass, which I use to measure my nap time, when a masked intruder wearing a monk's robe came in and attacked me. He wanted to know where we were keeping his **accomplice**, but I refused to tell him. He **tackled** me and tied me to the chair!«
The hunt for the second intruder began. Brother Donald and Flo, Philipp, and Caro were on the case. The kids wanted to investigate the abbey's old infirmary.
»Don't waste your time there,« Brother Donald told them. »The infirmary has been abandoned for years.«
Caro didn't believe him. She peeked through a dusty window.
»A waste of time? I don't think so,« Caro said triumphantly. »Someone was just here!«

**evidence:** der Hinweis; **grain:** das Korn; **accomplice:** der Komplize; **to tackle:** angreifen



**What made Caro so sure someone was just there?**

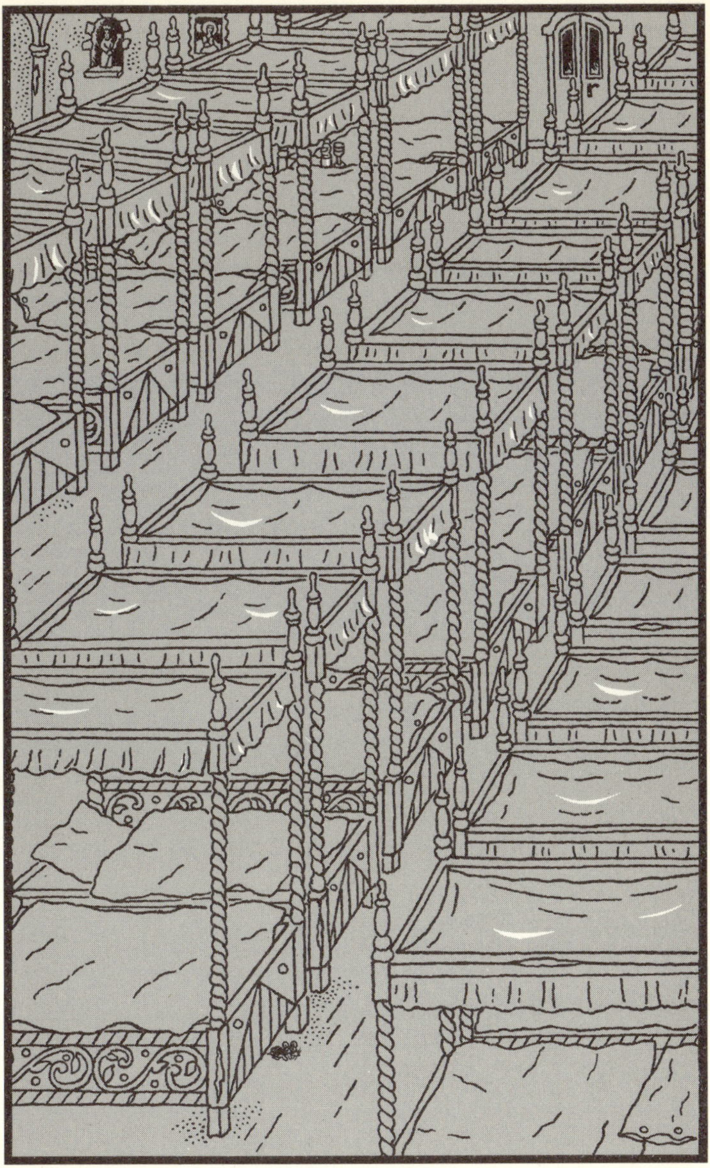

# 14. A Bloody Blow

In the back of the room, there was a half-filled glass of water on a small table. Flo deduced that this was where the thief hid before stealing the chalice. But where was his partner?
Philipp reached for the infirmary's doorknob when —*BAM!*— the door swung open and hit him right in the face. As Philipp cried out in pain, a man in a robe bolted from the infirmary and took off at top speed toward the emergency exit.

Brother Donald caught up to him, but the intruder spun around, tripped the poor monk, and took off. Flo gave his handkerchief to Philipp to clean up his bloody nose, and Caro helped Brother Donald to his feet.
»Burry up! Be've got to catch him!« shouted Philipp, his mouth **muffled** by the blood-soaked handkerchief.
»Don't chase him!« ordered Brother Donald. »It's useless to run after him. It might be better to set a trap.«
»Great idea,« said Caro. She showed Brother Donald a slip of paper she had picked up off the ground. »But the man trapped himself by dropping this piece of paper. He's planning to go to the circus tomorrow afternoon. What do you say, gang?«
»Let's go!« exclaimed Flo. »I'm sure I'll recognize him, even though I didn't see his face. There's one particular detail that will give him away.«
The next day, the three friends went to the circus's matinee performance. During the elephant parade, Flo elbowed his friends. He had found the thief's accomplice!

**muffled:** umhüllt

**What detail gave away the thief's accomplice?**

Calinero Circus
tomorro
3:00

# 15. A Tidy Solution

The man was seated in the third row, in the shadows. His face was buried in his program. Flo recognized him because while most men wear their wristwatches on their left hands, he wore his on his right. Flo had noticed this detail yesterday as they were chasing him.

»He probably had a meeting with someone, but who?« Caro wondered. »It can't be the thief, because Lars already arrested him.«

»Maybe it's the person who paid the thief to steal the chalice,« suggested Philipp.

The three friends hid near the exit of the circus tent. When the accomplice left the circus, the detectives would get him. But the accomplice knew what the detectives were up to. He hid among the crowd as hundreds of people poured out of the big top. The kids searched the crowd, but there was no sign of him. They were about to give up hope, when Philipp's face lit up.

»There he is!« he exclaimed. »It's incredible, he's already changed **disguises**. We can't let him get away again!«

**disguise:** die Verkleidung



**How was the suspect disguised this time?**

# 16. Breathless

After recognizing the three detectives, the phony street cleaner stuck his broom under his arm, grabbed his rolling garbage can, and started running away.
They followed the street cleaner to Fairgrounds Lane, where they saw him turn left at Alley Way.
»Hurry!« shouted Philipp. »He's getting away!«
»Don't worry,« said Flo, »Alley Way is a dead-end street.«

The street was indeed a dead end, but when they reached the entrance, there was nothing there except the garbage can and Coco the cockatoo, flying around. There was no trace of the street cleaner.
Suddenly, they heard a loud sound. Coco screeched. Caro, Philipp, and Flo jumped up, prepared to seize the **villain**. False alarm! It was just a cat that overturned a few empty bottles when it tried to get its paws on Coco. The detectives exhaled, but Coco was more **agitated** than ever. He let out another big screech and furiously flapped his wings. Philipp looked carefully at the scene and then turned to his friends.
»Coco figured out where the **fugitive** is hiding. This time, we've got him!«

**villain:** der Bösewicht, der Gauner; **agitated**: aufgeregt, aufgewühlt; **fugitive:** der Flüchtling



**Where was the fugitive hiding?**

Anno
12
1798
Fest

Anno
12
1798
Fest

# 17. The Fallen Angel

Philipp signalled to Caro and Flo to follow him. They **crouched** in front of the thief's hiding place and waited, counting the seconds. Exactly twenty-nine seconds later, the street cleaner's head emerged from the water barrel. Gasping for breath, he spat out a huge stream of water he had swallowed while underwater. Before the thief had time to make another escape, Philipp backed him into a corner with his street cleaner's broom.

When Leo and Lars arrived on the scene moments later, they found themselves face-to-face with a **soggy,** pale man whose teeth were **chattering**.
»Please,« he begged, »get this dirty broom off of me!«
The suspect accepted a handkerchief from Lars, wiped his face, and then tried to convince the detectives he was innocent. When Lars asked him about the garbage can, which was loaded with **precious** artefacts, he shrugged his shoulders.
»I'm a street cleaner. I sweep up whatever I see, whether it's valuable or not. I don't decide what people throw away.«
Caro decided to call his bluff. She fished a baroque statue of an angel out of the **trash can**.
»You're a very **thorough** street cleaner. You swept all the way to the abbey of Blackbird Rock!«
All the blood drained from the **culprit's** face.

**to crouch:** sich ducken; **soggy:** klitschnass; **to chatter:** klappern; **precious**: wertvoll; **trash can:** der Mülleimer (BE: dustbin); **thorough:** gründlich, sorgfältig; **culprit:** der Übeltäter

**What was the proof that the angel hadn't fallen from the sky?**

# 1. The Rabbit's Tale

It was the second angel, part of a matching pair that should have been alongside the organ at the Abbey of Blackbird Rock. The thief and his accomplice, who made their living **trafficking** works of art, were brought to justice. Father Anselm gave each of the young detectives a small hourglass as a way of saying thank you and Brother Donald made them a **raspberry tart**. The kids promised to keep in touch and visit again next year.

Case closed – for now! The friends hoped a new mystery would pop up soon for them to solve. Just their luck: It started that very afternoon at the town's annual **pure-bred** rabbit exhibition and show. The winning rabbit was awarded the Lapina Prize: ten times its weight in carrots and a yearlong subscription to *Raise My Rabbit* magazine.

After the show, Caro, Philipp, and Flo watched the crowd pass by the rabbits' cages from a nearby balcony. Flo took his binoculars out to admire the rabbits. Suddenly he cried, »Hurry! Someone just broke into one of the cages!«

**to traffick:** Hehlerware verkaufen; **raspberry:** die Himbeere; **tart:** das Törtchen; **pure-bred:** reinrassig



**Which cage is he talking about?**

ELEVATOR

## 2. A Bitter Victory

The three friends pushed their way through the crowd and stopped in front of cage number 873. Caro investigated the **padlock**.

»Flo is right,« she said. »Someone stole this rabbit! Look, the lock was cut!«

»And this is the rabbit that just won the Lapina Prize!« Philipp added.

»How do you know?« asked Flo.

»All you have to do is read,« Philipp explained. »I can even tell you what the rabbit's name is.«

»Maurice the Magnificent!« Caro exclaimed as she read the **ID tag** attached to the rabbit's cage. »Hurry up, we need to tell security! With any luck, we'll be able to stop the thief before he leaves the show.«

A few minutes later, the exits were locked, and all the remaining people at the show were politely asked to open their bags for inspection. But not a trace, not a single rabbit food, was found.

»I guess now we have to find the owner and tell him the bad news,« said Philipp. »We should call him over the loudspeaker.«

»That won't be necessary,« Caro said with a big smile. »I can see him from here. All you have to do is look.«

**victory:** der Sieg; **padlock:** das Vorhängeschloss; **ID tag:** *Abk. für* identity tag = das Namensschild



**Where is the owner of the stolen rabbit?**

Lapina Prize
EXIT
JURY
First Prize
Mr. Trenton's
Maurice
the Magnificent
SALE:
3 BABY
RABBITS
Healthy
Food
Especiall
for Rabbi
Raise
My Rabbit
Special Edition

# 3. A Discovery

**O**n the sign announcing Mr Trenton's rabbit, Maurice the Magnificent, just outside the arches of the hall on the left, you could see Mr Trenton's picture. Flo recognized him by his round glasses and big mustache. He was sitting at a big table in the back of the room with the competition's judges. When he learned about the theft of his beloved Maurice, Mr Trenton **clutched** at his heart. His bushy mustache started to **quiver**.

»If I catch that thief,« he **vowed**, »I will make him eat an entire box of carrots, leaves first!«

»My friends and I will do everything we can to bring Maurice back alive,« Caro pledged, tears **brimming** in her eyes.

Mr Trenton's face softened. »That's very nice of you, kids. I don't think Maurice's life is in danger. The thief probably just wants to resell him. Maurice is worth a lot of money, you know.«

Philipp showed Flo a little piece of paper that he had picked up from the bottom of Maurice's cage.

»I think this is a piece of the label of a fancy bottle of olive oil,« Flo explained. »Look, here's half of the label. It has some weird symbol on it. It must be the brand's logo.«

Flo found a copy of the Yellow Pages and wrote down the addresses of all the gourmet shops in town that sold specialty olive oils. The next day, they visited all the shops that they found. As the detectives studied the window of the third gourmet grocery store they had on their list, Flo cried, »Good work, Philipp! We found the right bottle!«

**to clutch:** ergreifen; **to quiver:** zittern; **to vow:** schwören; **to brim:** überfließen



**What is the name of the olive oil in question?**

Anthony LaSalle
Canal Groves
3.90
from Italy
Basil-Infused $7.50
Cold Pressed
This Rack 5 for $95
Fiery Pepper $20
Thyme-Infused
Special Blend $7
Perfect Olive
Olive Nectar
SALE
Fancy Rose Oil
3K Press
Ashland Grilling Oil
Lakewood Oil
Green Olive Oil
$59
Patron's Mark
Extra Virgin
BIKE
Fruity Oils
Pale Olives

# 4. Down the Rabbit Hole

Flo stood on his tiptoes to see what Philipp had found on the very last shelf of the gourmet shop.

»Fiery Pepper Oil, twenty dollars,« he read from the bottle. The logo on its label exactly matched the label half they had found in Maurice's cage.

»You don't actually think that this gourmet shop has something to do with the theft, do you?« Caro asked. She was beginning to think this whole idea was a little **ridiculous**, and she wanted some time to think. »Let's go have a meeting at the Sugar Shack.«

The boys reluctantly followed her out of the store. But before they reached the Sugar Shack, the boys stopped in front of a poster advertising a horror movie. As Caro told Flo and Philipp to hurry up, she noticed something strange. She took out Flo's binoculars from her backpack. No, she wasn't dreaming. Caro called Flo and Philipp over.

»Oh, wow!« said Flo, looking through the binoculars.

»That's incredible!« added Philipp, taking his turn.

»You were right,« Caro admitted.

Thanks to pure luck, the **investigation** was back on track.

**ridiculous:** lächerlich; **investigation:** die Ermittlungen



**What did the three friends discover?**

1892
Page-Turner-Bookstore
HOT
Boxing
7 o'clock
ZOO
Theater
"The Masked Devil"
BOOK SALE
Gloria Kino
NEW
Gallery
Circus
MISSING
555-5112
P.Roth

# 5. Crunched!

**A**mong the packages stored on the back of the **mail truck**, Caro saw a big box labelled »Fiery Pepper Oil«. And that wasn't all! Looking through Flo's binoculars, she noticed that someone had punched lots of little holes in the top of the box – air holes to allow an animal to breathe! There wasn't a moment to lose!
**Trapped** on the other side of the street, they watched helplessly as the **mailman** picked up the box and carried it away. He disappeared behind the door of a building. The light turned green and the friends ran across the street. They walked up to the door of the building where the mailman had disappeared.

»Now what?« Flo whispered. »We can't ring every doorbell, can we? Philipp, what are you doing?«
Philipp had discovered a tall ladder in the corner of the building's courtyard and placed it against the wall of the building. They climbed the ladder and peered into the window to their right on the second floor. They saw a dentist at work, but no evidence of Maurice. Next, they looked into the window on the left.
»Get down from there, you **rascals**!« the landlady of the building screamed.
The three detectives scrambled down the ladder. They had seen enough!

**mail truck:** der Postlaster (BE: post lorry); **trapped:** gefangen; **mailman:** der Postbote (BE: postman); **rascal:** der Lausebengel

**What did they see in the apartment that proved that Maurice was still alive?**

# 6. A Man Goes Shopping

»Phew! That was close,« Flo said once he was sure that the landlady wasn't following them.
»Let's keep going,« said Caro. »Maurice is being held prisoner in the apartment we saw through the window. I'm sure we all noticed the half-eaten carrot on the kitchen floor. Now we know that the thief lives in this buil-«
She stopped speaking abruptly. She saw that the door of the building had opened. Out walked a man wearing a hat. In his left hand, he held a picnic basket and walked toward the center of town.

Philipp, Flo, and Caro followed a little bit behind him, very careful not to let him see them. After a while, the man entered a sporting goods store. Through the store window, the friends watched as the man selected a backpack, paid for it, and put it in the bottom of his picnic basket. He left the store and continued on his way.
But the street was so crowded that the detectives lost sight of him. They decided to split up so they would have a better chance of finding him, and planned to meet up again in five minutes at the flower shop on the corner.
»I know where he is,« Flo said, once the detectives met up again after searching for the man separately. »Come quickly!«



**Where did Flo find the man with the hat?**

AMT

Magical Bread
Delicacies
FRESH SEAFOOD
Fruits & Vegetables
Fine Cheeses
LEGUMES
Flowers
Vinegars and Oils

# 7. It Moves!

»Here are your carrots, sir,« the grocer said to the man with the basket. »Anything else?«
»That's all,« said the man. He paid for his food, and walked away from the fruit and vegetable stand. The three detectives decided it was too risky to follow him back to his apartment, so they took a different route back to his building. They arrived there before he did, so they waited in front of the Sugar Shack.

»There he is!« Caro whispered as she spied his reflection in the window. »He's going into the building.«

»Great,« said Flo. »Now what do we do?«
It was a good question. No one answered. The friends were out of ideas.

»Wait, he's coming back out with his backpack!« cried Philipp.
The friends crossed the street and followed the man onto a bus. His backpack appeared to be **wiggling**! The man got off at the second-to-last stop, next to a farm that was near a forest.
Caro and Flo got up to follow him, but Philipp stopped them – the farm was so isolated, it would be obvious that they were following him. They stayed on the bus until the last stop, and then got back on the bus going the other direction toward town.
When they got off at the stop by the farm, they saw a fence surrounding the entire **property**.
»I see evidence of hungry bunnies!« said Caro peering over the fence.

**to pretend:** vortäuschen; **to wiggle:** wackeln; **property:** das Anwesen



**What proved that there is a rabbit living here?**

52
Larkin Farm

# 8. The Rabbit with Little Polka Dots

Two beautiful pumpkins grew at the back of the yard, and one of them had been **nibbled**!

»Okay,« Flo said. »So there could be rabbits at this farm, and they could have eaten the pumpkin. That's nothing extraordinary, right? How do we know the man brought Maurice here? Plus, I don't see any rabbits.«

Caro and Philipp suddenly **dashed off**. »Hey! Wait for me!« Flo ran after them. He caught up with his friends just as they approached a hole in the fence. Philipp looked through it. He began **to chuckle** when he saw the crowd of happy rabbits on the other side.

»Come look, Flo. I don't think you'll be disappointed.«

Flo crouched down and looked through the hole in the fence. »Wow! I've never seen so many bunnies in one place! They're so cute! And all different! Do you have the picture of Maurice, Philipp?«

Philipp handed Flo a newspaper article with Maurice's picture. The three friends looked very closely at the photo. Then they looked at the rabbits one by one, until they came to an agreement. Maurice was certainly there!

**nibbled:** angeknabbert; **to dash off:** davonstürzen; **to chuckle:** kichern, glucksen

**Where is Maurice?**

Where is
Maurice the Magnificent?
Nightly News
First prize winner oft the "Lapina
Prize" competition of domestic
and farm rabbits, Maurice
the Magnificent
in crowded room
his cage had been
trainer Sylvester
Serpol
over
reward
find the prize winner. The police
do not habe one suspect

# 9. After Much Consideration …

The rabbit in the photo had three blacks spots on each side, black ears, and a black tail. And he was sitting at the far end of the yard, **sniffing** a **drainpipe**.

»Let's see if he responds to his name,« said Flo, calling him quietly. Maurice turned toward Flo.

»Hooray!« yelled Caro, patting Flo on the back.

»Don't celebrate yet! How are we going to get him out of here?« Flo asked.

»Easy! We'll sneak in and grab him,« said Caro. She started to climb the fence, and the two boys followed. The confused rabbits watched as the detectives dropped onto the soft grass on the other side of the fence. The kids looked around to make sure no one saw them, then carefully moved toward the kidnapped rabbit. Caro reached out to grab Maurice, but he became afraid and slipped out of her grip. In three hops, Maurice disappeared into the barn.

»It's going to be difficult to find him in there,« Philipp whispered.

»Shhhh!« Flo interrupted him. »I hear footsteps.«

The detectives quickly hid behind some giant sacks of potatoes. The footsteps came closer and closer to the barn. Flo turned to Caro and whispered, »I know where Maurice is hiding! Look closely and you'll see!«

**to sniff:** schnüffeln; **drainpipe:** die Regenrinne



**How could Flo tell where Maurice was hiding?**

# 10. Coco and the Rabbit

Caro looked everywhere, but she could not find Maurice. Flo pointed him out: He was hidden in one side of the old and broken **scale** on the table in the back corner of the barn. Flo saw the tops of Maurice's ears, and noticed that his weight had made the scale tip.

»Achoo!!!«

The friends jumped. Someone had sneezed very loudly from just outside the barn door. The three friends peered out the doorway. The man with the hat putting his handkerchief back in his pocket was...

»Larkin!« Philipp exclaimed, remembering the name written on the sign outside the farm.

Coco **cawed** loudly. »Shh! Coco! Be quiet!« hushed Flo. The cockatoo ignored him and chased Maurice, who had left his hiding place and hopped off to join his bunny friends.

»What now?« Caro wondered.

Philipp replied, »If Larkin is hiding Maurice here, he must be waiting for money.«

»You mean he's looking for someone to sell him to?« asked Flo.

»Or he's already found someone,« Caro declared. »I think Larkin may be negotiating with someone right now.«

**scale:** die Waage; **to caw:** krächzen

**What is Larkin doing at this exact moment?**

## 11. In the Shadow of Bear Rock

Philipp and Flo looked where Caro was pointing. Larkin was on the telephone.

»Oh, look, he hung up,« Flo said. »And he looks really happy. He must have gotten good news. He's putting on his hat... Look out! Hide!«

The detectives **dove** behind a pile of wood as Larkin headed toward their hiding place. Luckily, he passed within inches of the detectives without noticing them.

»Let's get out of here,« Philipp said, and they ran past Larkin and up to the house. They peered through the window. On the table by the telephone, they saw a handwritten note. It read: »Five o'clock. The zoo.«

Flo looked at his watch. »It's 4:43 now, so the meeting must be tomorrow.«

The next day, minutes before five o'clock, the detectives waited outside of the Hillsdale Zoo with Leo and Lars.

»Your trip to the farm wasn't exactly legal,« Lars grumbled. »Don't do that again, okay?«

The detectives nodded as they entered the zoo. They paused at the top of the pathway that led to the sea animals' **tank**. Leo asked, »Do you have any idea where Larkin is meeting his friend?«

»Um... not really,« Philipp admitted.

»Look!« Caro cried. She was spying through her binoculars at Larkin walking through the zoo. »I see Larkin! And look at the man next to him! Don't you recognize him?«

**to dive:** hechten; **tank:** das Becken



? **Who is Larkin talking to?**

Five O'Clock The Zoo
WELCOME

# 12. The Carrots Are Cooked!

The detectives could not believe their eyes: The man with the big mustache standing with Larkin between the bears and the lions was none other than Mr Trenton!

»That's unbelievable!« cried Flo. »What a liar! Do you remember how upset he pretended to be when we told him that someone had stolen Maurice? Come on, let's hide and confront him when the moment is right.«

The detectives, Leo, and Lars tiptoed closer to the two men and hid behind the bear's rocks. They could hear Larkin and Mr Trenton's conversation perfectly. The two had been plotting together: The theft was staged by Mr Trenton, who wanted the insurance money!

»You've done a very good job,« the group overheard Trenton say to Larkin. »I'm pleased with your work. And don't forget! When Maurice becomes a father again, I want the three prettiest baby bunnies.«

»I won't forget,« said Larkin, taking the suitcase Trenton handed him. »Goodbye!«

This was their chance! The detectives sprang from their hiding place. Larkin sensed the danger and ran away, but Trenton froze with fear. Lars apprehended Trenton and led him out of the zoo. He locked him in his **squad car** and went back to join the others as they **chased** Larkin. The group found Larkin high in a tree overlooking the elephant building. Larkin had already hidden the suitcase filled with money somewhere else.

**squad car:** der Streifenwagen (BE: police patrol car); **to chase:** jagen

**Where is the hidden suitcase?**

1909
AQUARIUM
ELEPHANTS

Larkin left the suitcase filled with money in the elephant building before climbing up the tree. And it was filled with rolls of **quarters**!

»Not very practical to carry, but harder to trace than **bills**, which have serial numbers«, the police officer at the station explained to them after the friends turned the thief over to him.

Philipp, Flo, and Caro planned to take a break from their lives as the best detectives in Hillsdale, but only for now! Who knows what other exciting mysteries were in store for them?

**quarter:** der Vierteldollar; **bill:** der Geldschein (BE: banknote)

# Vocabulary

A

**abbey:** das Kloster, die Abtei
**accomplice:** der Komplize
**agitated**: aufgeregt, aufgewühlt
**aisle:** der Gang
**ajar:** angelehnt
**to alert:** alarmieren
**assailant:** der Angreifer, die Angreiferin
**to assemble:** sich versammeln

B

**balm:** der Balsam
**to be banged up:** mitgenommen sein
**bill:** Geldschein **(BE: banknote)**
**blackbird:** die Amsel
**to bolt:** sausen
**to brim:** überfließen
**broom:** der Besen

C

**candy:** Süßigkeiten **(BE: sweets)**
**caw:** das Krächzen
**to caw:** krächzen
**chalice:** der Abendmahlkelch
**challenge:** die Herausforderung

**to chase:** jagen
**to chatter:** klappern
**to chime:** läuten
**to chuckle:** kichern, glucksen
**to clutch:** ergreifen
**cockatoo:** der Kakadu
**cockroach:** die Kakerlake
**competitive:** kämpferisch
**consciousness:** das Bewusstsein
**to corner:** in die Enge treiben
**to crouch:** sich ducken
**cuffs** ( = hand cuffs): die Handschellen
**culprit:** der Schuldige, der Übeltäter

**D**

**to dash off:** davonstürzen
**dawn:** die Dämmerung
**deduction:** die Schlussfolgerung
**disguise:** die Verkleidung
**distress:** die Verzweiflung, das Elend
**to dive:** hechten
**dormitory:** der Schlafsaal
**drainpipe:** die Regenrinne
**to drop by:** kurz vorbeischauen
**to duck out:** sich davonmachen
**dumpster:** der Müllcontainer

**E**

**evidence:** der Hinweis, das Indiz

**F**

**fugitive:** der Flüchtling

**G**

**gadget:** die technische Spielerei
**to get in a flap** (*coll.*): in helle Aufregung geraten
**gooey:** zäh
**goosebumps:** die Gänsehaut
**grain:** das Korn
**grappling hook:** der Schraubhaken

**H**

**to harass:** belästigen, nerven
**haystack:** der Heuhaufen
**herb garden:** der Kräutergarten

**I**

**ID tag:** Abk. für *identity tag* = das Namensschild
**imposter:** der Betrüger
**infirmary:** das Krankenzimmer
**intruder:** der Eindringling
**inventory:** die Bestandsaufnahme
**investigation:** die Ermittlungen
**investigative wheels:** hier: der Spürsinn
**ivy:** der Efeu

**L**

**loot:** die Beute

**M**

**mailman:** Postbote **(BE: postman)**
**mail truck:** Postlaster **(BE: post lorry)**

**mayhem:** das Chaos
**medieval:** mittelalterlich **(BE: mediaeval)**
**miscount:** der Rechenfehler
**monastery:** das Kloster
**muffled:** umhüllt
**musty:** muffig, modrig

**N**
**nibbled:** angeknabbert

**P**
**padlock:** das Vorhängeschloss
**pants:** Hose **(BE: trousers)**
**passageway:** der Durchgang
**to perch:** sitzen
**phony:** falsch
**pillar:** der (Gewölbe-)pfeiler, die Säule
**to pop out:** hinausstrecken
**potted:** im Topf
**precious**: wertvoll
**prediction:** die Vorhersage, die Prophezeiung
**to pretend:** vorgeben, vortäuschen
**property:** das Anwesen
**to prove:** beweisen
**to prowl:** herumstreichen
**purebread:** reinrassig

**Q**
**quarter:** der Vierteldollar
**to quiver:** zittern

**R**

**rascal:** der Lausebengel

**raspberry:** die Himbeere

**to reveal:** offenlegen

**reward:** die Belohnung

**ridiculous:** lächerlich

**robe:** die Robe, das Mönchsgewand

**S**

**sanctuary:** der Altarraum

**scale:** die Waage

**to scold:** schimpfen

**shrub:** der Busch, der Strauch

**sidekick** (*coll.*): der Kumpel, der ständige Begleiter

**skylight:** die Dachluke

**to sniff:** schnüffeln

**soggy:** klitschnass

**squad car:** der Streifenwagen **(BE: police patrol car)**

**to stammer**: stammeln

**to stash:** verstauen, verstecken

**storage room:** der Lagerraum

**stub:** der Abschnitt, Abriss

**to be a sucker for:** eine Schwäche haben für

**suspense:** die Spannung

**T**

**to tackle:** angreifen

**tart:** das Törtchen

**temple:** die Schläfe

**tiny**: klein, winzig

**tiptoe:** die Zehenspitze

**thorough:** gründlich, sorgfältig
**to traffick:** Hehlerware verkaufen
**trapped:** gefangen
**trash can:** der Mülleimer **(BE: dustbin)**

**U**
**unconscious:** bewusstlos
**unpleasantness:** die Widerwärtigkeit

**V**
**to vanish:** verschwinden
**vast:** riesig
**vaulted:** gewölbt
**victory:** der Sieg
**villain:** der Bösewicht, der Gauner
**to vow:** schwören

**W**
**to wiggle:** wackeln
**woozy:** benebelt

## Julian Press –
# Finde den Täter

Spannende
Such- und Ratekrimis
für alle
Wimmelbildspezialisten

Finde den Täter
**Operation Goldenes Zepter**
128 Seiten, ISBN 978-3-570-13081-0

Finde den Täter
**Tatort Krähenstein**
128 Seiten, ISBN 978-3-570-13082-7

Finde den Täter
**Der Fluch des schwarzen Schützen**
128 Seiten, ISBN: 978-3-570-13083-4

Finde den Täter
**Aktion Gelber Drache**
128 Seiten, ISBN 978-3-570-13084-1

Finde den Täter
**Geheimbund Rote Koralle**
128 Seiten, ISBN 978-3-570-13233-3

10 006/5

www.cbj-verlag.de